Liquid Mercury Girl

2019

Dedication

For all those who love the power of words and their ability to "make the world finally stand still." For Erika who taught me to steer toward the pain. For my much-loved friends and family including Allan and Marcia Butterfield, and Shirlee Davidson. For William Samuel Nowlin and Glenn Pittell, who walked on from this world way too soon but left a multitude of intangible gifts for those fortunate enough to have intersected their lives. Most of all, for my my beloved and incomparable parents, Allen and Dolores Broyles, who have also walked on but not without teaching me to love, particularly those who only seem unlovable, and who who made me realize the healing power of laughing, though sometimes inappropriately but never with ridicule, as a part of our shared human experience.

Liquid Mercury Girl

Marianne A. Broyles

FIRST EDITION, 2019

Liquid Mercury Girl
© 2019 by Marianne A. Broyles

ISBN 978-1-7323935-4-7

Except for fair use in reviews and/or scholarly considerations, no part of this book may be reproduced, performed, recorded, or otherwise transmitted without the written consent of the author and the permission of the publisher.

Cover Art
© 2019 by Kindra Swafford

Author Photo
@ 2019 by Susan Riddle Duke

Interior photographs by Joseph Allen Broyles
& Marianne Aweagon Broyles © 2019

Mongrel Empire Press
Norman, OK

Online catalogue: www.mongrelempire.org

This publisher is a proud member of

COUNCIL OF LITERARY MAGAZINES & PRESSES
w w w . c l m p . o r g

I am here to liberate words from the solitary confinement of the dictionary and turn them on the world, so that the words stand upside down and the world finally stands still.

—A veteran with schizophrenia in the last days of his life

Contents

ONE

There Is	1
Aberration of Starlight	3
Prescription	4
Hypnogogic Hallucinations	5
The Scars	6
No Keys	8
Vacancy	9
Alpha and Omega	11
Liquid Mercury Girl	13
Potential Hydrogen	15
Transference	16
Refuge	17
Summer Camp, 1978	18
Swimming Lessons	21

TWO

All My Senses Search the Ocean	25
The Power of the Girl Scout Sash	27
42nd Birthday	29
Parochial Elementary School	31
Diego's Ocean	33
Independence Night	35
Ajar	37
Surprise Interruption	38
The Crazy on My Shoulder	41
The Heavy Coat	43
PTSD	45

Goodbye, Love	46
The MARTA Rail Preacher Takes a Gold Line Car	47

THREE

The Small Hours of the Morning	51
70 x 7	53
Eating Hibiscus	54
Elegy	55
Passenger	57
Hiawatha Asylum for Insane Indians	59
Heart Transplant	61
Second Shift	62
You Know That Feeling Then	63
Clearing the Way	65
Going Out to Sea	67
Iliana	69
Train Bound	71

ONE

There Is

No innocence
in the way
I touch your sleeve
however lightly
as if the cotton pressed
between my fingers provides real
leverage and balance in this
healthcare wasteland of
scissors and post-it notes
pens and white-out.

It is better to forget
all of it was built
on the backs of those without
power or birthright—
you with your
pale moon-scrap hands
and fading boyish freckles
and me with deep
Mississippi brown eyes.

And I imagine
beyond these ratcheted
gears of profit
some family I never
met with sun
glint beneath their skin

tenderly gather
roadside turtle shells cracked
by traffic on an Oklahoma toll road.

They will scoop out unfinished
lives and fill their clean
empty homes
with river stones
to shake transcendent music.

Aberration of Starlight

The scientific definition=the angular shift in
the apparent direction
of a star
caused by the orbital
motion of the Earth

Or reaching for you
deep in the night
To find you were never there.

Prescription

I've been told if I were good, and prayed for love,
and waited for it like a revelation, using
the index of the Bible to find what I need—
I might find you.

But there is magic that won't deliver.
You may never love me.

Still, I leave a pomegranate
on a white plate
beside your computer
like a blank prescription
because you'd told me they are good luck
but you'd never known how to eat one

So I instruct you to take a knife,
divide it like a brain's hemispheres,
sever electrical impulses to stop messages
to its other side, like an
eternal disconnect between reason and desire,

then knife it into quarters
like a heart's chambers

before you sink your teeth
into the seeds.

This may be biblically inappropriate—
but makes more sense to me than any
scriptures I've ever read.

Hypnogogic Hallucinations

Is what the psychiatrist calls them
unreal sounds and visions
tossed salt floaters
in front of half-open eyes
specks of memory like you standing
by a row of sunflowers in front of Kelly's
that smile only for me though you
were surrounded by so many
your devotion evident in the way
your feet and wide shoulders were set
your blue eyes so singularly intent
only on me in this St. Patrick's crowd
and then I am fully awake, fully aware
this is not real and another day has passed
but the pain is not less
like they keep telling me.

The Scars

In the quad and all over campus you sweet-
talked me into your twenty-year-old goddess
and though I didn't always feel comfortable as you
fawned over my eyes and hair and body
I believed you.

So that night, tipsy
from cheap college wine,
it was time to trust you enough
to unveil the scars
across my back the braille
of rainbow prisms that stitch
me alive
my whole self
that what I saw as shipwreck or splintered
plank my mother, my safe place,
called *beautiful*.

You didn't try to hide your shock
as your fingers moved across them.
What is that? you asked, flipping the light.
I watched your eyes as I transformed before you:
girlfriend to a form much less
desirable.

I tried to explain them with
nervous laughter.
They are the reason I'm alive
my voice retreated into itself—
Didn't I tell you about the heart surgery?
I could have died at twelve.

They really turn me off, you answered. *I'm sorry. I can't lie.*
And you cut off the light.

When your breaths deepened into sleep, I
covered myself in clothes, found my way
back to Woodruff Hall in the two a.m.
darkness. The just-planted saplings
held up by poles struck me
as heartbreaking as your words
spilling as black ink. Blood thick. And curdled.

No Keys

It was meant to be a simple thing when I casually
said hi but sometimes hi turns into something else
and that's what happened this morning when Mr.
Adams said he wasn't hi and he didn't have the hi's
he had the lows 'cause he was in this place where
the lows lived and there's really nothing to say
cause I got the keys to go out and come back
in the morning and a sky-blue car and some
money to spend on the way home and shoes
that fit and people who call me back and I'll inhale
fresh air and look at the stars for as long as I want
and my black and white dog will sleep by my feet
and lap the cool water I give her as I set my glass
on the bedside table and wait for sleep as the wind
rattles the rose bushes until I hear your voice in my head
I don't got the hi's I got the lows cause I'm in this place
and I ain't got no keys to live.

Vacancy

My patient's roommate is gone today, his bed
on the other side of the room
is fresh and made up and the window
over the bare nightstand could not absorb any more quiet.
No more conversations back and forth—laughter between twin beds
let loose like a kickball.

Usually, the one left is grateful for the solitude, but not you.
You can't sleep and ask for extra blankets.
The room is too cold now, you say. *My roommate went home.*

It was his breath from the other side that kept it warm.

Alpha and Omega

At the traffic light, I stare into my electronic
alter ego until it drops to green and I look up to see

two deer, four flame torch eyes
unexpected and ethereal

on the yellow line of a slushy highway
but nothing could sully their beauty.

We acknowledge each other.
A breath.

Then they leap away
from my car horn's gentle warning.

I pray they know to go
where the earth is soft.

Liquid Mercury Girl
For RMC

You told me again of you and the sisters next door
kneeling before your parents' rectangular hedges
up in Los Alamos. Each took a dime and held it close
as if it were a wafer at the communion rail,
and let it hover over the lawn,
waiting for the mercury to lift
from freshly cut grass
like luminous strands of hair.
You all pretended there was a beautiful girl
shaped by liquid mercury, whose movement was guided
by the dime between your eight-year old fingers
just below the topsoil, waiting for you to rescue her
from the ground like Persephone in Hades.
Sometimes at night you'd sneak out with the yellow cat
under a full moon illuminating those secret mountains
and the laboratory buildings ringed by chain-linked
fences and *Keep Out* signs where your dad
went to work with a silent sense of duty.
You could think of nothing better than
you and your yellow cat telling your secrets,
like Sam, the eight-year old
you loved before all others,
to your liquid mercury girl,
A hidden mirror of your spirit.

Potential Hydrogen

I relive our first kiss and I think of the pool
I loved so much, how I would always try to get
that duty, while my dad took the net and skimmed
the surface for stray leaves and petals
from last night's thunderstorm while I took to dipping
the litmus paper, testing the pH to see how it would lift—
pink, blue, purple—Was the balance right?
No longer gangly or awkward, I see you
driving up after your summer job and
imagine our tongues finally touching
so lightly like that litmus paper
dipped in the deep end of the pool.
Will they lift the same color?

Transference

For the man who remembers
The blue dress I wore last Tuesday
For the man who reaches to cover
My eyes when a yellow dog darts
Into the street.
But most of all, for the firefighter
Who gently moves me aside
To take over my burdens
When my mother has fallen again
And I don't know what to do other
Than stand over her
Contorted body.
This is why I wish, why I wonder
How I could lift his burdens.
How I could be so much more.
Most would say it's only a case of transference.

Refuge

While you practice swift water rescue in the Rio Grande
I want to be a blue heron keeping watch
or the relief of this cool river from desert
afternoon sun.
I want to be the currents you ride when
you're tired and need to gather energy.
I want to be the underwater reeds
fanning against your legs and
a patch of scalloped shore
to hold your footing as you
emerge from the water.
I want to be your deep breath
of flowers closing on the twilight
that comes so quietly.

Summer Camp, 1978

I was learning to shake it at eight
at the Methodist Cheerleading Camp,
something my mother didn't like
even though she signed all those
permission slips.

But there I was
shaking it to "Night Fever"
on borrowed pom-poms
until mine arrived in a box
that seemed way too skinny
for what was inside—
blue and white pom-poms,
the very same batch, we were told,
as the Tiger Cheerleaders.

Opening the box was disappointing.
What was supposed
to be blue and white pom-poms,
full and transformative,
were two limp things, lying there
like dead squid over styrofoam
crushed ice.

I remember this tonight as
we walk through
downtown Albuquerque
in crisp skirts.

You pause to light a cigarette,
fumbling through your purse
searching for your lighter like a lost word
when a window
slides down and some frat guy
yells *Whore!*

which cuts us
like a cook filleting fish,
spreading each side open until together
they become wings
floating over soft white flour.

Swimming Lessons

Our bodies are mostly water
so there is no room in mine for more.
Not even when the swimming teacher
prodded us forward to the concrete lip of the pool
and announced it was going to be okay
and we had to do it so I jumped in like I was told

and I realized my feet wouldn't
touch the ground and it really wasn't okay
because I was flailing my arms
and gasping as water
muffled air.

As the other children watched in shock,
I watched their bodies become halves
bobbing and thrashing
until she decided I really couldn't do it
—that white-capped devil—

and lifted me like a carcass from the water
where I coughed and sputtered chlorine

trying to rise like a water hyacinth in my throat.

TWO

All My Senses Search the Ocean

I know nothing better
than the first touch of foam
against my legs when
the tide comes in.

She is the grandmother
I did not meet but know
her living DNA
moon-dusts my bones
as lines of gentle swells

lift me away from this earth
for only a second or two.

But that is enough
to glimpse its horizon—the edge
of a porch door to my mother's house
where she patiently waits
for her family to come home.

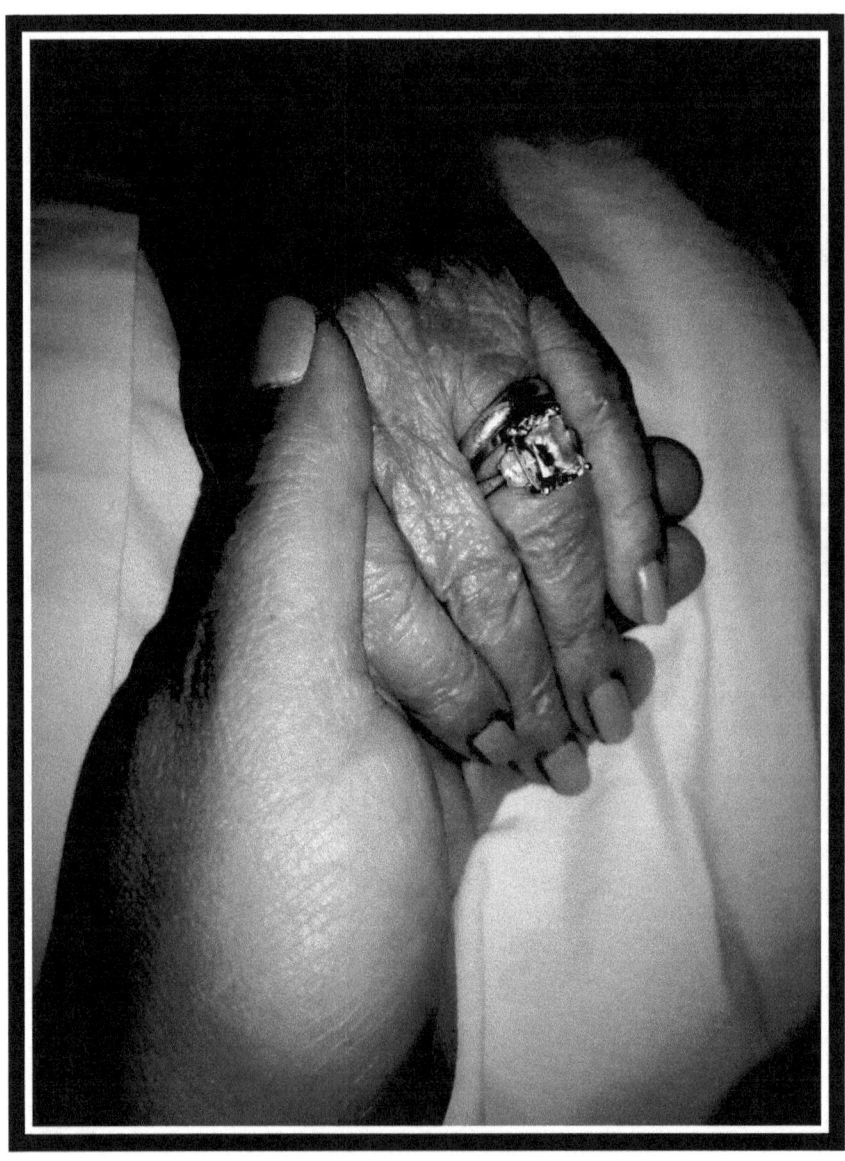

The Power of the Girl Scout Sash

At eleven, I wanted to be
alongside my father

no matter where he went, I'd want to be—
even if it was the Paducah Funeral Home
to visit the bereaved.

He'd walk me past the room with all the coffins
to the break room where the funeral
directors could laugh.
They'd tell me jokes and buy me
a glass bottle coke, frosty from the machine
the carbonated liquid fizzing over the lip
with the hiss from the bottle opener.

If I had my Girl Scout uniform on,
with its ambassador-like sash,
I'd feel especially proud and stoic,
knowing my endurance must
somehow be bettering America,
maybe even giving strength to the grieving.

At the very least, I believed my sash
festooned with pins of honor
was my vaccination against death.

And I would never have to lie in a
satin-lined coffin with my hands folded
around a cross when I had my sash
and my father to protect me.

42nd Birthday

I began to study the art of being mean at seven.
Though it was scorned by my parents,
it was a necessary tool
I would need, like my dad with his
well-worn hammer,
To defend myself from those barb-tongued
church girls between Sunday school classes.

They always sat in the balcony
where I was not allowed to sit.
Practicing meanness did not feel good, or right, or decent.
It sometimes made me feel sick
but it never failed them—

In the summer I was seven and learning
the art of being mean,
my Aunt Julie was diagnosed with lung cancer, then bone cancer,
then blood cancer, then everything cancer. Half
of her chestnut curls were gone by July. She couldn't bear
to see them in the brush, something visible falling

off her body, so she'd rip tufts out of the bristles and throw
them in the trash, every morning and every night,
unable to look at herself in the mirror.
Still, she bought a dress for her birthday. It came in the mail

all the way from Sacramento,
where she had grown up, where she
had been on welfare and could barely
spend money on herself even now.
But she found the spirit to buy a blue Grecian dress
for her 42nd birthday.
When the doorbell rang she and my mother
hovered over the box,

quietly exclaiming as if they expected
something living inside
and wanted to comfort it.

They took scissors to its taped edges,
lifted it open, and parted the white tissue
to reveal it was the color of the Pacific
halfway out on the horizon.
She lifted it out, carried it to her room,
and emerged in it draped over her so elegantly,
despite her thin arms and patches of hair.

What do you think, she asked, looking at me, her beloved niece.
"I think it's ugly," and turned away from her as my syllables hit

her like small arrows.
My mother gasped "Marianne,"
drawing in her breath in horror.
Aunt Julie started to cry
and I felt my heart contort
as I turned away from her.
I wanted her to hurt as much as I hurt, for knowing
she was going to leave me, leave us, very soon,

probably before the first frost in Connecticut and
all the ocean-blue dresses in the world
couldn't change anything.

Parochial Elementary School

Geometric with ramps and squares
and rectangles of stained glass,
hidden crosses. I made a C in Bible,
disappointing my teacher by
repeatedly confusing the order of its
books. They all knew my father
was a minister and I should know better.
Paul, a Greek Orthodox, was held
back in the second grade. We thought
he did strange things in his church.
Rituals. Paul and I passed notes while
our teacher met with her reading group castes—
the smart and crisp, the respectable yet
unremarkable, the slow and disheveled.
Paul and I were in the "second" group, and
therefore paired to hold hands for the
Christmas processional.
In chapel or at our desks, we excelled at
fervent attention. Our heads bowed in unison
when the teacher turned off the light to make
us quiet. On career day, they asked us to
pray about our careers. It was Friday afternoon
and we were getting restless when Bobby Thomas
declared that his brother wanted to be a policeman
and he wanted to be a robber. They escorted Bobby
to the third floor to be whipped by the principal
so he would learn to
hate crime, the way all good
Christians do.

Diego's Ocean

You tell me if you could you'd transport yourself to your childhood

in the LA projects. They were unique, you say, like no other

projects in the world. You could see the ocean from your bedroom

window. It was bad, the gangs and all that, but you had the ocean.

And when it was too much for even you, you'd go

to the rooftop and listen to the Pacific's waves

cresting and breaking, cresting and breaking

just the crescendo of your name

Diego, Diego

Then, ahead of schedule,

all those projects were razed,

and there was lots of money to go around

so you had to go somewhere else, some other

projects deeper in the city

but no amount of money could stop the ocean

from searching for you

Diego, Diego

Like a teacher pausing at your name

while calling roll to the back

of an empty classroom.

Independence Night

Many people cannot wait for the sun to drop
and night to fill with erupting chrysanthemums
exploding orbs
sparks dissipating in the horizon
flashbulbs in our vision.
But for you it is different.
You tell me you hear bombs, grenades, gunfire.
Pyrotechnic colors mirrored in a river takes you somewhere
I only know from the news.
You crouch in your home,
covering from flying shrapnel,
closing the curtains on our celebrations.
This night has nothing to do with freedom.

Ajar

My father dying
left me skinless
raw and unprotected

My mother dying
pulled my muscles
away from me
My shiny resilience
flew to the sky
with her

All the most fragile
things I have live
in the least elegant
cage of bones

But only this feels true
(   )

Surprise Interruption

It started with a pigeon's muffled wings
in the TV room of the psychiatric ward.
The sound of searching,

    away,   away,   away.

We all look up toward the Styrofoam tiles
that frantic cacophony
audible over the local traffic report
blaring from the TV.
Patients watch the staff to see
if they hear it too
some looking grateful
for this common experience.

Jill slides a mammoth plastic chair
filled with sand directly beneath
the ceiling tile where the pigeon taps
unintelligible syllables, like a Navajo Code Talker.

She reaches toward this sound
removing the dusty tile, reaching in,
lifting it from its dark mine
and holding it as if it were made of crystal
for presentation to a high-ranking official.
Her fingers are deep blue velvet wrapped around

its heaving, feathered body.
And its eyes are two perfect ink drops
quivering on a sheet of white paper
like Jell-O salads carried on a cafeteria tray.

After the stillness of terror, he beats his wings
against her hands until he is just tired
enough to take a respite from fighting,
resigned to accept whatever fate he has.

Jill marches toward the back patio door—
A small procession of patients and staff behind her
to witness.

Her hands open and he lifts off
with all his strength,
feeling an entirely different
sense of surprise.

The Crazy on My Shoulder

landed when they were wheeling
your body out in a paisley shroud
you would have never worn in life.

The crazy on my shoulder
is a mockingbird or a catbird
you sometimes said was song

language I could not understand
all the questions I never
thought to ask you or even worse

forgot.

The Heavy Coat

I try to resist need for you
like I tried to resist the heavy
winter coat my mother would
drape around me
the same way she covered our canary's cage
at night so he would sleep instead of sing.

I remember my mother molding me
in layer after layer of clothing that stuck to me
like newspaper plaster of Paris in the wet cold
of Boston rooftops veiled in clean powder
that surrenders to gray slush of the streets

as I surrendered to my mother—
until I whipped off the scarf
then gloves and stocking cap
my grandmother made.

Thirty minutes of pure freedom
spinning on playgrounds, dangling
from monkey bars, that cold
metal shock more defiant than my will.

And today you are my freedom
to remove what is too heavy,
what must be tossed to the ground.

There will be time to retrieve
whatever it was
like spinning wool of daily living—
getting up, working, making money,
trying to please, trying to heal others.

That time is not now.

PTSD

My patient tells me when he got back
From Afghanistan
He couldn't stop taking four showers a day
Scrubbing himself
Until his skin reddened, desperate for moisture
As the Arabian desert.
He said his girlfriend
Didn't understand
Why he could take so many showers
When he hadn't even gotten sweaty
Or dirty in the first place.
This made him feel even farther from her
Than the oceans and continents
That separated them before.
He said I could not tell her
The horrible things I did like when
I was leading a convoy through a village
And there were all sorts of people there
Doing their work for the day.
Children chasing a hoop or kicking
A homemade sad, unraveling ball
Laughing and screaming
I wanted to stop so bad knowing
What was going to happen
But my Sergeant
Put a gun to my head and said
If I didn't follow orders he'd
Shoot me right there.
So I did it.
I did it and I will never forget.
I keep scrubbing my body
In the shower under water as hot
As I can stand and then some,
Thinking it might help wash death
Out of my pores
The blood splatter off the windshield
While my girlfriend sits in the bed
Twenty feet away from me.

Goodbye, Love

When I open the door and Raina is there, I look into her face
as she told me what only seemed unspeakable,
"They found Glenn's body this morning."

(And my life will never be the same)

Shock transforms me into a child in our small Maine kitchen.
My father is at the sink choosing from the styrofoam
bucket an unlucky mackerel to gut.
He lifts one out, flips it over, it thrashes wildly.
I pray not to glimpse its eyes in time to see
them dim. There is no sound, only the smell
of death from their soft white bellies as
he takes the knife and starts at the throat.

(Oh God I can smell it again)

Now my dad goes straight down the middle,
not showing emotion, a true fisherman,
it splits so easily, like jelly.

(Yea though I walk through the valley)

Its guts, the color of beets.
Dad runs cold water from the faucet—water
we're not supposed to drink because it tastes bad
and we're downwind from the nuclear power plant

(Surely goodness and mercy shall follow me)

The beet-tinged guts whisk down the drain
(Oh Jesus, what have I done?)

and there is only an empty mackerel
(All the days) (of my life)

The MARTA Rail Preacher Takes a Gold Line Car

On the Gold Line MARTA to Doraville
he gets on at College Park, does not take a seat
or grab a bar to keep his body from rocking
with the train. Instead he holds a thin stack of
white fliers, begins to hand them out like
funeral parlor fans at an August church meeting, but it
is not hot and most cast their eyes down,
fold their arms close to their bodies
like two burning logs behind the fire grate
that is the aversion of their eyes,
away from this transient interruption in
this subway car.
*If you all could take a minute for God and follow along
with me keeping in mind Proverbs 13:20 as I read ...
Paragraph One ... Everyone can't be in your front row...*
His voice booms, rises and falls with a preacher's inflection
as we fly from the inner city out toward the suburbs on the
Gold Line to Doraville. Then he stops, pauses.
*I'd like to take this time to see if there's anyone here
who wants to be saved. Does anyone want to be saved here today?*
I wait, wonder if anyone is going to let him save them on
this MARTA rail car. One man covers his mouth, laughing.
But the MARTA Rail preacher is unwavered, goes around one by one
to see if anyone wants to make a small donation
for printing costs. I take the handwritten paper of
those who can't be on your front row and
hand him five bucks.
The same man starts laughing again.
Then the train makes another rough stop.
Our bodies are flickering candles moving left, then right,
then straight and still again.
The door hisses open and the MARTA preacher
steps off, still beaming, his own altar, his own baptismal,
a dove beating in his chest
just one stop short from Doraville,
which is the end of the Gold Line.

THREE

The Small Hours of the Morning

My mother tells me April in Maine
is especially cruel—
So if the crocuses arrive early
snow blinds their
purple, yellow, scarlet, and
tangerine eyes emerging
through the ground.

And so it becomes true for me too
on that April 8th night, hearing
you left this world.

Oh that I could fold into myself
and let my end come too.

If only you'd waited out the night,
like most of us have done,
count the hours till daybreak,
when you have someplace to go,
when things seem normal again
if for no other reason than

your birthday is next week and
the shoes you wanted so much
are already in the mail.

70 x 7

How many of my palms will it take
to fill the space between the drawbridge
of your shoulder blades?

How many times is a bridge a safe place
and how many times do I want to lay
my body across it?

Eating Hibiscus

On a slice of cake
I imagine this will do beautiful things
as it rolls from my tongue down
the unlit staircase that is
my throat
in the body
that is my house, my house of
flowers tumbling
velvety petals, deep flush
of pink, nuance of perfume
and all else it is,
all else it implies.

Elegy

Cynthia told me soon
I'd dream about you and that would
comfort me somehow.
But I don't, really, except right
after you died
and you were leaving the grocery store,
wearing a bucket hat,
pushing an empty cart.
No one else seemed to notice.
Just the other day, though
I saw you in my half-asleep mind
in a blue doorway, moving farther
and farther away, from corner to
corner against the black until
you just disappeared.

Every night before my eyes close,
I wait for you to visit me,
stare at my white popcorn ceiling
expecting a meteor shower.

I remember that time we stood by
the Xerox machine
which was malfunctioning at the time.
As you opened one of its pieces like part of a mouth
to yank out a piece of paper
with a torn edge
You know I love you, you told me.

I let you go on, as if nothing had happened.

Your wife would have a private viewing before
the cremation. I wondered if I could get around this—
I thought of running to the funeral home,
begging some undertaker to
let me see your body even
though I was not an expected guest.
I thought of other more dignified things

I could do—walk in like I belonged
and had just forgotten the time,
and my name should have been on the list and I was running
late, I had a meeting, somewhere else to be ten minutes ago
after fulfilling my brief duty to my family.

As if you were my family.

Passenger

Great Aunt Mary fell
in love in Jersey—so her heart,
packed with newlywed love
and family wrath,
went to India on an ocean liner,
its name not recorded.

As the oceans warmed,
did she imagine this waiting
continent of lushness
and vivid colors?

Could she ever dream in years counted
in a small clump of pink lotus,
a fever would take her from two men
(one a part of her)

and then she'd leave that earth too
on wisps of burning cardamom and tears?

Hiawatha Asylum for Insane Indians

In Canton, South Dakota there are voices
Trying to speak.
They lie in a graveyard on a hill,
Their bodies tossed and planted like a packet
Of wildflower seeds that will never blossom.
They were sent from across the country in 1903
To this federal hospital—an asylum for insane Indians
Built with brick and mortar in the shape
Of a Maltese Cross.

They were sent for alcoholic dementia, chronic melancholia,
Congenital imbecility, and those diagnoses not recorded
Such as protests against the United States government,
Religious nonconformity, and poor adjustment to colonization.

I imagine most never danced again, never saw
The transformation of great open skies at moonset again,
Never felt the rush of cold Sioux River currents around
Their ankles or heard the voice of the person they loved again.

In Canton, South Dakota, there are voices trying to speak.
They have moved from one silent prison to another—
A graveyard on a hill surrounded by a golf course.
According to the documents, many outsiders do not know
They are even there, unless they hit their golf balls
Out of bounds.
Who will ever read the plaque on the wooden fence carved
With a list of their names—Big Day, Blue Skies, James Blackeye,
Silas Hawk, Edith Standing Bear, Two Teeth, and Yells at Night.
Who will know they even lived?

Their creator knows, the land knows, the river knows,
The deer know, the mice know, the owls know, the moon knows
And we know.
But what will we do with this?
This knowledge that is too heavy
For even the sweeping wind to raise?

Heart Transplant

Franklin is so tall and solid, I imagine his bones
Could stretch into a Redwood and his feet transform
Into a fern, barely touched by sun.
Behind heavy, black-rimmed glasses his eyes are dark,
Distant branches
While his heart is a bonsai, each beat measured
Like small cuts from pruning tools that stunt its growth.

I ask the questions of a psychiatric assessment to find,
In this moment, Franklin is not suicidal.
He believes he can go on living even if only
Because others count on him.

As I consider this, I place the stethoscope's bell
Against his chest and listen to his heart pump blood
As he tells me what no nursing text could ever teach—
The reason he cries more—
It's because I have the heart of a woman.

Second Shift

I'm so tired in my tenth hour I struggle not to forget
each tiny plastic cup of rainbow pills goes with a distinct
face that is a door leading to constellations of stories.

But it is the tenth hour of my fourth day
and I am so tired of hearing their
pain and think there will probably be a fire drill too

before the shift is over and what I want to
do right now is walk out of this place of plastic
wrap over food and gloves before touching

anybody and disinfectants like tears that form and become
hanging mirrored globes.
I want to rid myself of scrubs and become

unrecognizable.
Until then, will even the clothes in my closet
fall in love and make a striped family entirely

without me?

You Know That Feeling Then

My patient has carried almost all the books
And magazines from the psychiatric ward bookshelves
To his room down the far end of the hall.
Taking them little by little so no one will notice
Until they are all gone.
Most of the magazines are strewn across the floor
Torn, ripped, arranged for his own story.
The books randomly stacked in small piles,
Their meaning unrealized only to us.

I find him circling around them engaged
In conversation with the unseen.
I ask if he would mind sitting down to talk
For a few minutes, holding two green Haldol
Pills in a tiny plastic cup.
We talk about his voices and the date, his mood,
His pain, his sleep, his appetite.
And then we move on to talking about home.
His in Savannah and mine in Memphis.

You know that feeling them, from down home, he says,
And no additional explanation is necessary
As we find our center point.
He talks about things being so much faster

Out here, out West, flapping his arms
As if he's in a swimming pool and keeping
His head above water or trying to fly.

He says, *I like it like this.* Then he spreads
His arms out and I cannot help but think
Of the story of Jesus in His boat, calming the seas.

I ask him why thinks he is here. *I'm just waiting
To be called. I know they will be calling me soon,
So I'm just waiting here so I can fight the enemy
Whenever I'm needed.*

I thank him for telling me this.
Then he covers my hand with his large
Black hand and I am painfully aware
I hold a card he doesn't have—information
About his medications, his privileges, his tests,
His dispositions. And then he just says
I love you. You know that feeling from home.

Clearing the Way

From the balcony, all I see of Rocky Point on the Sea of Cortez
is its barely visible shape—the outline of a crouching black coyote.

When will night grow tired of its hunting and roll over to
expose its underbelly of gold, pink, orange, blurring into blue?

I discern the horizon from the ocean by a string of
lights that burn all night—the only way to know where one

world ends and another begins.

They shine like a jeweled necklace—a line of demarcation
separating a woman's head from her heart until

night backs away to allow the secrets of being, the hidden
juts of land, to walk into the morning.

Going Out to Sea

Uncle JL lived with a silver plate in his head
from World War II—a channel marker floating
in his brain's electric pathways.
So when the spring storms in Oologah would come,
JL would rise in silence from the kitchen table.
His family knew without asking.
They knew he'd go to the fields and walk through the crops
in the rain—the headaches so great he did not know what
else to do other than this, unless it was touching the newest fringes
of growth against his palms, watching gray clouds
floating through the Oklahoma sky
like glaciers on the verge of calving with
thunderous claps, freeing whatever was locked inside them.
And JL, his silver plate always with him,
pacing through his landlocked ocean pain,
of dipping barometric pressure,
winds picking up, distant lightening,
and finally the promise of dissipating rain.

**Oologah is a town northeast of Tulsa.
Its name is from the Cherokee language and means* **dark** **cloud.**

Iliana

You tell me she is in her place every summer, the same corner of the Chilean coastal resort. You and your family look forward to seeing her every year, give her some money when she stops to speak, to take a brief hiatus from ruling her territory, her own island of concrete.

Iliana, you tell me, leads her life in that pleasant, even affluent, vacation spot. People don't seem to mind her—they are used to her. She is a fixture even if she likes to scare children, lifting her arms as if to grab a trapeze wire from which she is about to fall, yelling at them in her schizophrenic tirade, showing them her teeth.

They scatter like tossed coins to the safety of their families. But most people don't really mind Iliana. No one calls the police, no one fills out paperwork for a peace officer to bring her in for a psychiatric evaluation because she is crazy and likes to scare children.

She is part of the continuum there—as much as tourists checking in and checking out of villas, espresso hissing all day, ice cream dripping on the beach, fisherman gutting sea bass for market, tossing them on a mound of ice, and the silent, microscopic work of our own cells dividing, regenerating, keeping us alive.

Train Bound

When I go home to Memphis, I stay in the hotel
by the train tracks, so I can hear the train rumbling by,
cutting through deep summer humidity, the moonlight,
the night stillness, the heat lightening
comes and goes like a mockingbird.
I can count on it.

Not like comfort.
Not like a man.
Not like another day.

I lie in bed, imagine its wheels
telling the tracks

Love now, love now, love now.

Acknowledgements

Poems in this book have been previously published in the following journals and anthologies:

"Vacancy," *Yellow Medicine Review*, Fall 2012

"Summer Camp," 1978, *As/Us Inaugural Issue*, January 2013

"Eating Hibiscus," *As/Us Inaugural Issue*, January 2013

"Heart Transplant," *As/Us Inaugural Issue*, January 2013

"Swimming Lessons," *De l'autre cote du chagrin: Anthologie de Poetesses Indiennes*, 2018

"PTSD," *De l'autre cote du chagrin: Anthologie de Poetesses Indiennes*, 2018

"Going Out To Sea," *The Florida Review Native Issue*, Summer 2010

Photo Credits

All but two photographs in this collection are used by permission of the photographer, Joseph Allen Broyles. The author and the Press thank Mr. Broyles for sharing his evocative images.

The photos that accompany "42nd Birthday" and "The Power of the Girl Scout Sash" were taken by the author, Marianne Broyles.

Marianne Aweagon Broyles first became interested in contemporary Irish literature and poetry while studying at Emory University with the late Dr. Frank Manley, a poet, playwright, and fiction writer whose titles include *Within the Ribbons* and *The Emperors*. After graduating from Emory, Marianne earned her MA from University of Memphis where she also focused on Creative Writing and was privileged to work with John Bensko (*Green Soldiers*), Brett Singer (*The Petting Zoo*), and Gordon Osing (*From the Boundary Waters: Poems*).

Marianne was born in Boston and raised in Memphis, Tennessee. She moved to the Southwest in the early 2000's and lived in both Albuquerque and Santa Fe, New Mexico. She is an enrolled member of the Cherokee Nation of Oklahoma and currently lives in Nashville, where she works as a psychiatric nurse. *Liquid Mercury Girl* (2019), by Mongrel Empire Press, is her second collection of poetry. *The Red Window*, her first poetry collection, was published by West End Press in Albuquerque in 2008.

www.ingramcontent.com/pod-product-compliance
Lightning Source LLC
Chambersburg PA
CBHW071239090426
42736CB00014B/3147